WHAT'S BETWEEN *YOUR* EARS?

By Joy de Pominville

DEDICATION

To anyone wishing to optimize their lives
by purging stinkin' thinkin'

LIST of the INNARDS

Chapter 1
WHAT *IS* BETWEEN YOUR EARS?

So what **IS** between your ears?

And are you satisfied with what's there?

I know what is between *my* ears is not always productive, useful, or even remotely interesting.

I am kind of known for multi-tasking to the nth degree much to the chagrin of others around me, making them agitated, hyped up, or not even vaguely envious of this ability to say the least.

Often my thoughts run amok deploying swiftly in many different directions. My mind is usually able to collate, sift, and prioritize fairly proficiently, but the operative word here is "usually".

I recently read that multi-tasking does not serve to strengthen one's focus, brain longevity or plasticity, thought follow-through, and ability to excel. Hmmm, I may be in trouble since I plan to live til 140 with acute faculties and perfect health.

I am about to share how I, and perhaps you, can work on a plan to change what's between the ears for the better.

The plan will always be a work in progress, but that makes life interesting, and change is the impetus to an active vibrant brain anyway, or so I am told.

Chapter 2
HAPPY HAPPY HAPPY

There is a lot of hype about being "happy" as a main contributor to less dis-ease, fewer mental issues or broken relationships, and general physical well-being.

So what exactly is "happy"?

It obviously is an inside job and not about walking around with a plasticized smile on your face.

It is a feeling that you incorporate in your whole being. Think back to instances when you felt genuinely happy or at-ease with everything around you, including yourself.

Perhaps it was watching a video of a mother elephant finally finding her lost baby and watching her running ecstatically to him, or reading a heart warming snippet about a soldier returning from war and surprising his family, or falling in love, or seeing a photo of someone rescuing a drowning cat in a river, or the smile on an older person's face when you surprise them with a visit.

These examples were probably fleeting and perhaps never recalled again but your body and brain always cemented that feeling.

Point of Reference?

But what if you don't have a point of reference? If say, you've never experienced sight because you were born blind, you have no point of reference as to what seeing is. Ahh, but even the blind have the other partners involved, the Mind and Spirit or Core of who You Are (I call it CYA). "Visions" pop up in the brain when something is described, or felt with the hands, and your CYA creates and embodies a definition just for you. You traverse through life with your own points of reality and references so nothing is lacking, just different.

For example, from trauma or drama, experiencing "happy" may not be in your repertoire of feelings. You grow believing you can't be happy, but your definition of "happy" is most likely based upon what you discern from other people, their experiences, media hype, stories describing bliss and nirvana. This emotion is totally personal and unique for everyone. Your "happy" meter is not the same as the next person's.

All emotions and feelings and sensations are learned and expanded. For example, charting a course to define "happy" could be a benign comment or phrase you heard that inexplicably made you smile or laugh, or an exotic scent from nature, a forest, a beach, mountainside, or perhaps the warmth of a sincere hug, anything that touches your soul in a way that provides you a point of reference. From there feelings can magnify, be explored, questioned, tested, and ultimately learned. There! You now have point of reference, a guidepost upon which to attach more experiences and models. Now the ball is in your court to do your add-ons.

Science has shown that cells always gravitate to growth and sustenance, not decay and lack.

Good feelings provide security, power, and help you thrive with high fives! They can be motivating and inspirational and have you craving for more. Not so good feelings leave you deflated, maybe angry, despondent, and depressed and ultimately a couch potato mentality with no drive or motivation.

So which feelings would you like to hone to enhance your travels through life? You can learn anything, just ask that Mind/brain of yours, it's pretty egotistic and lauds its virtues and talents.

We can pick our path of least resistance and forge the road of life until our expiration date. It is a choice to make that road interesting with detours, lively with people and nature, stimulated and challenged with obstacles to figure how to traverse.

Or choose another laid out road where one can plod along in drudgery on an already trodden trail with set grooves, without detours, very quiet, with the same views day after day, climbing over obstacles with minimal effort.

In the end, whichever road is chosen, how would you answer the question, Brandon Burchard, author and speaker poses, " Did I live, did I love, did I make a difference?" Your answer affects your "happy" meter.

Happiness is not something you *get* in life, but rather something you *bring* to life. It encompasses mobilizing how you want to feel. Being placid and waiting for "happy" or any other good feelings like peace, gratitude, serenity, wholeness, even independence to arrive knocking on your door to be let in, may result in one having to wait a long time.

A big hat tip to author Neale Donald Walsch in his Conversations with God books, relayed how to be happy was "to cause another to be happy and experience it because of you."

"Your life has nothing to do with you. It's about everyone whose life you touch and how you touch it. "

This friends, is gold so keep that thought in your noggin.

Chapter 3
BECOME IT

The trick is to *Fake it til you Become it,* as speaker Amy Cuddy coins this axiom.

The old phrase, *Fake it til you Make it,* implies achieving a certain state, like happy, but for me, it is transitory and fleeting. When you *BECOME* a feeling, like *happy*, you have it for life, as it automatically gets ingrained into your CYA (Core of who You Are). You can easily begin this process, and yes, it is a journey, by incorporating doing things to make *others* happy, such as surprise visits, sending an occasional thinking-of-you card, paying it forward, giving out small compliments, or offering little random acts of kindness, all without expectation for anything in return.

The brain is just a receptacle for all experiences, learning, encounters, and events in one's whole life and it never forgets. It can open old dusty folders from ancient file cabinets recessed kilometers down, despite state of the art padlocks or codes to open them, with or without our permission or request.

Since it is only a receptacle, we are the ones who attach meaning, inferences, opinions, judgments, and sentiments to what is in those files. We also connect dots to other files we consider relevant to access and expand upon.

Whaaat? I'm not perfect? Blame it on that monkey....read on and you'll see who he is.

Chapter 4
The MONKEY MIND

As we traipse along in our lives, we become quite adept at creating our own biases, judgments and personal conclusions. Often these are not even based upon all the facts, and we make assumptions without supporting evidence. It is easy to fall into this trap and justify these habits as probably self-protection and guarding tactics. Then we aren't sucked into situations we think are threatening or go against the status quo. It is a bit like self-preservation of our egos and what we individually define as living a good safe life where we are accepted and liked.

You may ask what's the big deal whether I keep these habits?
The answer really lies in asking the opposite, is there a disadvantage? A big YES to that question.

Embracing an objective, observant, and open mind, helps to squash a "monkey mind" where thoughts run askew, a bunch of what-ifs emerge, the mind rolls through its rolodex of info to make evaluations and usually assumptions.

According to Buddhist principles, the "monkey mind" refers to being unsettled, restless, or confused. Writer and Buddhist Natalie Goldberg, who teaches many writing workshops, suggests that the monkey mind is the inner critic and is connected to the ego, which contends that you can't do anything right.

She states it's also the part of you that stifles creativity and prevents you from moving forward with your passions. The monkey mind insists on being heard, and sometimes it takes a lot of self-control to shut it down. It is also the part of your brain that becomes easily distracted, so if you want to get anything done in life, your challenge will be to shut down the monkey mind.

I admit it can be challenging to squash these patterns and having thoughts run amok and still retain our uniqueness and CYA (Core of who You Are). The key is simply noticing when we begin falling prey to these habits , which is not as easy as you may think. Our responses have been learned and repeated; that's how a habit forms, through repetition. Un-learning a habit uses the same process of learning and then rinse and repeat, this time, learning something different.

 But you can't change something you aren't aware that you are doing. So how in heavens does one do *that*?

Chapter 5
STOP , LOOK, and LISTEN

The very *First* step to consider is the query, " are you happy with who you are?"

If the answer is yes!, YAY for you!!
If you are unsure or waffling, check whether the source for "not sure" is coming from your thoughts, maybe your physical body, or your spirit, which can have two meanings: your vitality or aliveness is one and the other is that inner sense of knowing you are in balance with everything around you, the people, decisions, environment, the activities you choose, family, the path you've chosen.

The *Second* step is acknowledging whether you
a) are satisfied with your happy level, or
b) want to improve your happy quotient or
c) are emphatic about a complete overhaul.
Whatever your decision, just jump over yesterday and move on.

If you chose b) or c) keep in mind that nothing is ever "wrong" with us. When things are fixed or static, they stagnate, and energy gets stuck. Stuck energy keeps looping and the physical body can suffer, thoughts and brain flow get disrupted, and the spirit or vitality sags. The only way to divert this stuck-ness is movement or action plus a desire to change direction.

It is not about thinking something is "wrong" with *us*. That is stinkin' thinkin'.

What is *wrong* could be our food, the soil, the air, a parenting guffaw, politics, toxins, a mis-guided statement, or some trauma. Those *wrongs* contributed to our perception that we are imperfect. We personalized these wrongs and concluded then that there is something wrong with us.

When we place that label on our chest for all to see, we forget to *hang up on our hangups*, as a good friend used to tell me. And regarding these "hangups", you are better off to get *over* them before you get stuck *under* them.

 As Bruce Lipton , author of The Biology of Belief, found, " as fast as you change your perception is as fast as you change your cells." "you can change the chemistry of your blood when you change how you see the world." And he should know, after all, his research and experiments unequivocally demonstrated this as fact.

Beliefs are choices. And as someone quipped, "Before you make up your mind, open it." Author Miguel Ruiz tells us that the mind can give up its stories, and we are all free to say "no" without penalty, "yes" without regret, love without limits and we are free to surrender to life.

So if you ponder improving your lot in life, make a different choice, pave a new road minus any ruts, and explore new possibilities. Add a big dose of curiosity which negates any fear by changing its perspective.

Once you consciously consider a new card dealt, your awareness of how you typically played your hand in the past seeps up and now you can plan out a new strategy to win this game called *life* with miles of smiles.

Chapter 6
CARE to BE AWARE

As mentioned, how we act, speak and conduct ourselves are based upon learned behaviors and are pretty much under the radar where we don't even notice our patterns. You can't modify something that isn't perceived. So how can we hone that awareness animal anyway?

Here's a tip for coaxing your brain to notice every time you pinpoint becoming *aware* of a habit you wish to curtail. We'll just name it *Flipper,* only because I like that name to remind me to flip my thought. You can give it any name you wish though. The point is like that idea of snapping a rubber band on your wrist as a negative aversion technique to help you stop doing some type of behavior you wish to stop.

Doing a *Flipper* is more of a positive reinforcement. Here's how it works. You say the word *Flipper* aloud (the best) or in your head if you are shy, but also say this and pair it with a tiny action. It could be snapping your fingers, or counting to 3 forward or backward, or rolling your eyes, or whatever you pick. It is like doing your own a self-hypnosis.

Try this whenever you catch yourself noticing that your response was judgmental, or you bungy jumped to conclusions, or noticed your mind was racing trying to find just the right comment or suggestion or solution, or you assumed the worst or best of a situation, just anything that signifies you are tapping into that darn monkey-mind again.

The goal is to flip that thinking by saying the word, Flipper, and the action solidifies the flip. This won't stop you from proceeding down that monkey path, but it *does* solidify your awareness that you were heading that direction. That's the goal. The more often you do the flipperooni you begin laying down new asphalt on a new road.

Once you are accustomed to the Flipper, you can advance to the next stage.

Chapter 7
THE CHANGE IS COMING

Change the meaning you give things. You can turn your fears, anxieties and self-put downs inside out. How do we do *this*? Now it can get exciting and creative, heh heh.

I'll give you for instance. Say you have a fear of public speaking, and you are scheduled to present to your workgroup. Your palms are already sweating, and your throat is closing up.

In place of that fear, make up a story to tell yourself that you were *specially* chosen to offer some great ideas and input towards solving a problem, making changes manageable for others, and visualize your whole audience as being helped by your contribution. This is a fable you tell yourself, and remember to Fake it til you Become it. You have the editor's supreme right to change the narrative of a story your brain tells you is true.

Chapter 8
JUST GET IT OUT

It is said that depression is the lack of expression. Always bottling up your opinions, views, or secrets tends to squash the spirit. As the saying goes, "sharing is caring", and this does not just apply to material things. Of course there is knack to learning how to express yourself without being obnoxious, rude or insulting, but that is the easy part.

The difficult part is actually exposing your feelings so people around you discover you are in fact just like them, with all the flaws, with nooks and crannies stuffed and asphyxiated with dramas and traumas and what ifs and definitions you coined for yourself, blah blah blah.

Stuffing is not just for turkeys, and we are not turkeys. It is an art in which we can opt to either excel in creating, making it more spicy or bland by adding ingredients, *or* spoon it out bit by bit, digest it, preferably with some wine, and slowly lessen the amount.

Chapter 9

MONKEY BUSINESS FALLOUTS

WORRY: Zig Ziglar quipped that this infamous demon, Mr. Worrywort, "is interest paid in trouble before it comes due". And who likes trouble anyway, especially if it hits you where the good lord split you.

WHAT-Ifs: They are ghosts from the Past and villains from the Future who try to steal your thunder in the Present. Surely you don't want a "what if" at the end of your life…. A tad bit late.

ANGER: Anger is one letter short of DANGER. Useless to poke this sleeping tiger.

See if you can replace one emotion with a different one, just for a minute. Snap your fingers to wake you up and of this rut, then force a smile or hiccup or cough or from some other bodily part just to grab your attention to do a switcherooni and pull you out of *danger.*

WHY MEs and POOR MEs: Victimhood in all its glory coming to haunt you. When we can take responsibility you cannot be a victim. You are then in the driver's seat. Stand up to stand out. Amy Cuddy in her TED talk shared, " Your body language shapes who you are". She suggested assuming a power posture for just 2 minutes can change your life. Standing up straight, tall, with arms outstretched like Wonder Woman may just change your image!

They say emotions are merely Energy in Motion. So they need Movement up and out to be expressed. A good friend wrote that "feelings are like breathing, they come, and they go out."

Open the door so any feelings can come and go as they please. If the door is shut, the bad ones are trapped, but also the good ones can't come in. Be selective and on-guard.

Now you deserve a break at this point so just give yourself a hug and rub your hands up and down your arms. This is a technique called Havening that calms the fight, flight, freeze responses. Who knows whether this info is making you crazy, or appeasing your senses, or causing some grief.

The skin has receptors and rubbing your arms soothes these nerve receptors normalizing the immune system. So onward soldiers to the next part.

Chapter 10

USE

USE: Sometimes known as "what's the use" which is a defeatist approach pointing the way to uselessness and apathy, both signal an on-coming demise of your CYA, (Core of who You Are). Loss of independence can trigger this word too and can begin a spiral to less movement (you recall that emotion is energy in motion, and the less energy spent leads to sluggish and dull and eventually inert emotions.)

Here's the time to look in the mirror and get into gear, pull your boot straps up, and kick yourself to action. Spur that creative mind we all have to fortify your USE before it slithers into Use-LESS.

Aging, or physical mobility issues or loneliness or even resentment can be waste products of over comparing. You reflect on what you *used* to be able to do, places you easily navigated to before, or tasks you were able to complete effortlessly and independently and compare the past to your present state.

Well, la-di-da. Life is a journey and the itinerary changes, with or without your permission. Take inventory of what you *can* do, rather than what you *can't* do. Wallowing in the past and worrying about the future cannot gift you with the gift of the present.

Stretch those neurons in that amazing brain of yours and you can flash on a myriad of things you can do. Picking up the phone and calling a friend to make their day, learning a new hobby online or making an appt. with some young kid to teach you, or learn how to surf the net which can open whole new worlds of information to tax your brain and whet your appetite with new ideas.

Organize card games, mobility exercise groups online, yoga (a yoga teacher in a live group was 95 yrs. young), start weight training with water bottles (they say that preserves muscle strength, which you can do while preserving that brain muscle).

Go ahead, you can still be creative, and if you tell yourself you aren't creative enough, you are right... hint hint.. do that switcherooni with your words and thoughts.

Chapter 11
THE TRIO

There is the magic trio of body, mind and spirit, which many cultures, even faiths, conventional and non-conventional thinkers and writers agree to this triple link. The connectedness of these 3 meld together and create one "self", or oneself. If one-third of this combo begins to suffer or lags behind or loses its vigor, the other players also begin the decline. Can't be helped. They are stuck at the hips forever.

Ensuring all three are at optimum performance can be challenging at times, but merely recognizing when one participant needs a hand up is all it takes. It is just honing awareness and good observation skills like detectives. Practice makes perfect too.

So thoughts, physicality, and the Core of who You Are, (you recall my shortcut is the CYA), some call this your spirit or soul, are partners in crime. Any one of these can derail the other, so the big job is to keep them all in line, have them communicate freely all the time, notice the answers, and all will be fine.

Our prime mission is the most difficult, and that is, to *REMEMBER* that there are 3 constituents working together continually. Consider them one entity with three interwoven units, like a sweater has sleeves and body and a neck. Can't be called a sweater if one part is missing!

Chapter 12
THE PARTS OF THE TRIO

Your Mind

To know you is to love you and to love you is to know you. Works both ways. If you aren't clear on who you really are, not the person you want others to think you are, then how can you honestly love the real you? When you sincerely love yourself, you *will* know who you are.

The knack is to love who you *are,* then... love who you *were*. Now you've completed the circle and are whole again.

It is a mind game. And we all know mind games can be thought-provoking, inspiring, intriguing, trying and maybe even tricky. Who doesn't love the occasional mind game, like yellow school buses, to rev you up?

Develop your own personal Mind Game. Yes, it falls in the category of an Awareness Game, but it can reap a ton of insight and benefit to the other 2 players in the Trio.

See if you can play the *Catch Me If You Can Game*.

When and if you find yourself making an assessment of yourself that is negative through the words you speak, the faces you make, the way you carry your body, the thoughts that crowd your head, and even the aches and pains you may have, pull out the Catch Me If You Can Game.

All you need are 2 competitors, you, being one and the other being the negative assessment, which you can give it a name to be more entertaining, like Doofus for example.

The object of the game is to see how many barriers you can place between yourself and Doofus, your negative whatever, before he catches you. Once you get to 3, you are Safe. It goes like this:

For example Doofus is a phrase you use , "I'm not good at meeting new people."

Some of your barriers you can put up before Doofus can catch you, (and yes, you do have to have skin in this game and have to really come up with your own ideas), may be:

-----When I was a baby, I met a ton of people and I even smiled at a bunch.

-----I've bumped into a lot of folks on buses or in stores, even said, "excuse me", and even though they were strangers, they accepted my apology.

-----When I was in grade school, I did make friends with some classmates.

-----(Bonus) At a party once, even though I didn't speak to anyone, some people came up to me and said hi and offered me a drink and food. They didn't run away screaming either.

These counter your Doofus phrase.

Another example: the Doofus phrase is " I'm not a good cook".

What episodes in your life countered that?

-

-You made breakfast in bed for your mom on momday and she didn't puke.

 I can make myself a hearty breakfast and a good sandwich.
-I make lunch for my kids.
To what are comparing yourself?: a Michelin star chef?, your grandmom's Sunday casserole?, a cake your neighbor made you for your BD?

What we say to ourselves is our own belief from a comparison we've made to who knows what. And when we can put a full stop on comparing ourselves, what peeks out is an authentic, honest and matchless you.

Soooo were *you* caught by Doofus?

Your thoughts are what shape you. There is a popular belief that genetics and family histories are major determinants for how your life may unfold. Dr. Bruce Lipton in his book The Biology of Belief again, completely disproves that, and scientifically, since he *is* a renowned cell biologist and was a professor at Stanford.

His contribution to epigenetics, which is the study of how your environment and behavior play a significant role in how your genes work, completely overhauled the teaching world. Your individual DNA profile of what makes you is not changed but how your body *reads* this DNA sequence can be changed and that is what defines you.

You always have choice. You can tweak your habits, change your environment to minimize physical and mental stressors, and create an internal and external milieu that supports you to flourish, and display your best you.

Yes, Martha, you are not doomed by your past. You can divert dis-eases to never be expressed and yes, it's all in your head. Put that gem between your ears!

Your Body

Got any aches and pains? Or what someone else coined a dis-ease and flipped that coin on you?

Or had a little accident curtailing a body part for an interim, or even a big accident, sidelining you for even longer? Or caught a bug that you can't squash?

You don't have to believe me, but everything happens for a reason, and nothing happens out of thin air, even if you are hiking high up on Mt. Kilimanjaro.

The body always knows everything. It gets signals from your brain when your diet isn't right, or if you are overindulging in habits which are damaging, or ingesting ingredients that are poisonous. Messages from your brain go off track and sometimes cannot find the right pathways for muscles, organs, bones, blood and cells. Cells get confused and get stressed, and they try to send you signals to tell you something is wrong. You just need to listen with your inner ears, your second brain which is your gut, and do a quick review of your habits.

Our minds change our bodies. Again the reverse is true: Our bodies change our minds.

The body can't listen when the mind is busy because it cannot receive the messages clearly and goes off the reservation towards illness. The body CAN self-correct if given the right elements

When our diets are lacking, foods are engineered, unnatural additives abound, the needed elements and nutrients to over-ride any imbalances from invaders and toxins are insufficient and don't allow the body to self-correct.

Same goes for negative thinking and beliefs which has science-backed evidence that illustrates these affect your genes, your blood, your organs.

Your physical you is also very sensitive to the thoughts in your brain that pop up giving you hints to guide you to figure out what it needs, is lacking, is veering you off the correct pathways. The body likes to be in charge, but it takes direction from the thoughts that poke through and prod you to investigate.

 So if you are thinking, "woe is me", or "I am always a sucker for bugs that are going around" , or "I 've always been accident-prone", or " I can't help my genetics", then the brain says ,"yes, ok, whatever you say, you are right". Afterall the brain is only the repository of data and information and the body, who is the control freak, acts on the messages delivered.

The hint here, is to slowly become aware of what's been showing up. Yes, it's that Awareness guy again.

It could be a similar comment you *happened* to hear from two separate sources, or repetitive things happening often or in tandem, or an article *you just happened to read,* or new info you *happened to hear* from the radio, TV, seminar, media or friend. The clue here is what catches your attention.

The next step is to do something different about what's been popping up. Oh heck, be daring, and review the info as if you were a third person observer. You may just get a new perspective and the light will shine on a new action plan. Then it is up to you to decide whether to follow through or stagnate. Remember Einstein's adage, Insanity is doing the same thing over and over and expecting different results."

There is a great book titled, "The Body Never Lies by Alice Miller". Read it, it's true. And as Bruce Lipton surmises on that same line, he believes "our biography determines our biology."

I'll throw this in as a BIG HINT. Two undercover superstars who have amazing transformational abilities to create astounding make-overs to your biography to allow changes in your biology, are named, *FORGIVENESS and GRATITUDE.* Invite them in.

If you start with your head (making some additions, subtractions, deletions, even divisions and multiplications), your body will follow. The body is a patsy for a strong leader. Taking inventory of what is going into your body and checking the box either good, bad, or indifferent will give you a final tally of how your body is responding to the intake. Then you can logically decide your plan of action.

For those computer heads, a good analogy I read is to: Think of your body like the hard drive and the mind is the software. Every thought must be processed in your body.

"Imagine a population of trillions of individuals under one roof, in a state of perpetual happiness- such a community exists. It is called the healthy human body." (Bruce Lipton).

What an example of *happy*!

Your Spirit or Core of who You Are (or CYA, my word)

Can you put a finger on the CORE of who YOU ARE? You can point to your brain and your body, but the Spirit or CYA is ethereal and nebulous, secretive yet divulging and serves to also CYA (other meaning.. cover your a--).

It is all-knowing and is a master observer and watcher over the interactions between the other 2, the mind and body. You can't hide anything from this guy. He is non-judgmental, is a seer into the future, and fiercely protective of you from when you began as a teeny stem cell and slowly developed into a masterful *persona*, intact with your own unique blueprint.

Despite being understated and discreet, he is **THE** main character of this Trio. He is the behind-the-scenes director, overseeing all that emerges from the other members.

When the other two, the Mind and Body, are calm, compassionate and considerate of each other, are aware of what is missing and seek to fulfill any missing links and strive to create an equilibrium above and beyond the call of duty, CYA blossoms. He also retains a didactic memory and never forgets a thing. Darn!

CYA also really does CYA (cover your a--). He is like a sandwich, oozing with love, which covers you both from the back and the front, always preserving your distinctive essence. Keeping you safe and acting as your buttress upon which to fall back on are his main jobs when those other 2 seem to be struggling.

He gives subtle hints via intuition, miracles, instinct, happenstances, or twists of fate to help guide you to be your best YOU. But you have to hush that mind first, then open the heart, and then he lays out all kinds of answers, solutions, and revelations for you in a cornucopia of possibilities from which you can choose. Your role to have skin in the game is to have **Trust** that nothing is hopeless, unsolvable, irreversible, or the end of the world, unless of course it really is the end of the world as we know it, and then wow! that would be exciting!

The Soul /Spirit/or CYA supplies the license for total Freedom, allowing you to express the real you. How can you distinguish the real vs. the fake you?

The Fake You:

-runs through life pleasing others over number 1(you),

-takes jobs that may be profitable and estimable but just cause you stress, the kind that gives you indigestion, headaches, insomnia, bad moods. (all not good for trio members 1 and 2).

-is stingy on smiles and laughter, giving and receiving

-rarely pursues what really floats your boat

-can't devote time to check in and observe and re-evaluate the path you are on

-has excuses for not indulging in special treats, trips, adventures, occupations

-experiences fallout from Trio members 1 and 2

Now **the Real You**:

-contributes to all Trio members being in sync, and identifies on-coming conflict signs

-identifies ASAP which one needs a wake-up call and tweaks whatever feels off.

-is aware of invaders who can steal any member of the Trio's joy and quickly installs a barrier

-is confident there is always Hope, a solution for problems, and

-knows that stress comes in two forms, good and bad. Good stress like exercise, pushes the body to move which is a free antidote to all dis-ease. Immersing yourself in a project that excites you and incites you to create something fun and rewarding is also a good stress

Breath holding exercises like physiological sighs give gentle stresses with big benefits. (Patrick McKeown' books The Breathing Cure and The Oxygen Advantage delineate the hows).

Then there is bad stress of which we often fall prey to, like mental stress from work, family breakups, poor habits like smoking or over-drinking, poor diets and sleep. Well, we all know what these do to our bodies, our faces, our **C**ore of who **Y**ou **A**re!

The TRIO is so intertwined that when one is off kilter, it affects the others, but when one is in Olympic shape it also affects the group.

It helps to *remember* the Trio is a team effort to keep *What's Between Our Ears* aligned with our best interest, to **Trust** the Trio will always have your back, is destined to succeed, never deserts or abandons you, and never leaves you to face any adversity or challenge alone.

Chapter 13
PUTTING IT ALL TOGETHER

When you quiet the Mind, you can open the Heart. Works the other way as well. When you open the Heart, it quiets the mind and guess what? this combo totally escalates the real Core of who You Are (CYA). And how?

When you stop that mind chatter, that monkey mind again, the "quiet" in the Mind allows pathways to open new ways of thinking, flashes of insight, alternate solutions to "live by design, and not by default" as the saying goes. A few minutes of reflection blocks out all that ambient noise that engulfs us all day, sending its tentacles to irritate and rub raw the brain cells clawing its way to find repose and want to shout, "give me a break!"

If you ever had doubts about the existence of the CYA (or spirit), chew on this.
Ever wonder about things like:
-spontaneous remissions of diseases where poof they just vanish into thin air?
-or the source for instincts?
-or the stories of how prayer resulted in positive outcomes-especially from a group?
-or how hands on healing techniques, or practices like reiki, or mind over matter, or distance healing, or animal communication work?
-or even times when you were just thinking of someone and they happen to call that day?
-or telepathy communication?

-or-things we term coincidences without confirmed bases.

-or effects of meditation?

-or levitation, and not the kind you see in magic shows.

-or events like ability to bend spoons or walk over burning coals (which I have personally done and had nary a burn scar!)

-or how people in a group can resonate with a particular frequency from yawning, or laughter, or even sadness and then begin exhibiting those same frequencies?

These are examples in my mind of the essence of the Trio combo at its best.

Here's an article I "happened" to come across as I was penning this section.

"Emphathosphere- intuition, coincidence,, telepathic think of someone and they call:

A Nobel Prize in medicine was awarded for the discovery of "an inner GPS in the brain," but while we now know this faculty of the brain affects how we map our surroundings geographically, could it also guide us in other ways?

Theories building on this discovery take us into the realm of intuition and "coincidences." When you bump into just the right person at just the right time, could it be some kind of internal global positioning system (GPS) seated in the mind at work?

Norwegian researcher Edvard Moser, his wife May-Britt Moser, and British-American scientist Dr. John O'Keefe found that "grid cells" in the brain comprise this inner GPS."

OK, this is a bit technical and "scientific" for me, but it serves as an attempt to explain phenomena. I'm still at a loss to reason why humans seem to always search for tangible scientific explanations and not settle to *Just Be*. Sometimes it really is what it is with no further explanation necessary. Adopt trust, sprinkle in a degree of belief, and have gratitude for the opportunity to witness "miracles", which are everyday happenstances.

These examples can all sound pretty woo-woo but distinctively real It is akin to how all those millions of processes combine to have the human body coalesce and create an incredible system. Same with nature and examples of plants talking to one another warning of impending danger or disease (yes, it is real, look it up), or the wonder of nature period! Or the makeup of the Universe and the unknown beyond our planet.

Your CYA in all its intrigue, offers a tenet to live by. See things as happening TO you vs. FOR you. TO us is where we can take stock of what is coming our way, evaluate which ones to embrace or repel or discard or remold. We are in control. All these things are gifts.

Viewing things as happening FOR us implies someone or thing outside of you is steering the ship and we give automatic license for it to show up. Holding the helm yourself lessens the chance to become a victim.

Garth Brooks, country singer, has lyrics: "some of God's greatest gifts are unanswered prayers". We can plead, shout, ruminate , wish, meditate and pray for something to come to us, but perhaps there is something out there attesting to that tenet that things happen FOR us, rather than TO us.

When life is not FUN, bring WISDOM, and when
wisdom fails, bring PATIENCE, and when patience
is in short supply, bring ACCEPTANCE, and when
acceptance is difficult, bring GRATITUDE, which
reverses negativity and from there we've found
PEACE.

Author Neale Donald Walsch

\

Other books by me:

Pure Joy Living.. and Horses
Pure Joy Living for Kids
The ap-Parent Chef
My Super Hero Cian
If I Had a Do-Over
Allison and the Sleepies
Manners Matter
Goodies for your Moodies
The Little Book of Zoomies
Heart Bits to Keep You Well
Baby Talk